Tipu Sultan

Sunandha Ragunathan

Tipu Sultan

First Edition: July 2009
64 Pages
Printed in India.

ISBN 978-81-8493-192-1
Pro-ya-en-45

Prodigy Books
177/103, First Floor,
Ambal's Building, Lloyds Road,
Royapettah, Chennai 600 014.
Ph: +91-44-4200-9603

Email : support@nhm.in
Website : www.nhm.in

Contents

1. Hyder Ali ... 05
2. Tipu the Tiger ... 15
3. Tipu Sultan's Early Military Career ... 18
4. Tipu Sultan the Farsighted Ruler ... 26
5. The Nitty Gritties of Tipu Sultan's Rule ... 29
6. Tipu Sultan – a Villain or a Magnanimous Ruler? ... 36
7. Tipu Sultan the Diplomat ... 44
8. The Third and Fourth Anglo-Mysore Wars ... 48
9. Tipu Sultan's Advanced Weaponry ... 52
10. The End of Tipu Sultan and the Very First Resistance ... 60

Hyder Ali

The most prominent figure that springs to the mind of an outsider when he thinks about 'India' is Mahatma Gandhi. Gandhi was instrumental in shaping and making India. Our freedom struggle possessed unique ideals and methods which has even inspired other nations to freedom.

However, in our freedom struggle which spanned a period of over 200 years, there are many unsung heroes and heroines. One of them is Tipu Sultan (also spelt as Tipoo Sultan). A pioneer in our freedom struggle, his stand against the British happened as early as 1799 when he died fighting for his city.

Tipu Sultan – Sultan Fateh Ali Tipu – is also known as the Tiger of Mysore. He was the de facto ruler of the Indian Kingdom of Mysore from 1782, with the death of his father, until he met with his own death in 1799.

Aren't you curious as to how Tipu Sultan earned the name 'The Tiger of Mysore'? It is said that Tipu Sultan was hunting in a forest with a French friend, when he came face to face with a tiger. His gun would not go off, and his dagger fell to the ground as the tiger jumped on him. Tipu managed to reach for the dagger, pick it up, and kill the tiger with it. From then on, he has been referred to as the Tiger of Mysore. He also had the image of a tiger on his flag as his banner.

When writing such biographies, it is often hard to separate fact from fiction and truth from legend. It is possible that Tipu's subjects, caught in the fervour of nationalism, might have glossed the truth inadvertently. Nevertheless, it is important that we know that his title The Tiger of Mysore may not have necessarily originated due to his wrestling a tiger. We could perhaps take solace in the fact that though there may not have been this real tiger that he wrestled with his bare hands and killed with his dagger, we do know for sure that he fought the allegorical tiger in the British and defeated them several times in numerous battles!

Tipu Sultan was the first son of Hyder Ali. Tipu Sultan was a learned man and an astute soldier, and was also reputed to be a good poet. He was proficient in Urdu, Kannada, Persian and Arabic. He was a devout Muslim. Though the majority of his subjects were Hindus, they were his staunch loyalists as he was a benevolent ruler.

A good statesman, he had political and military alliance with the French. At their request, he built a church, the first in Mysore. In the struggle against the British, both Tipu Sultan and his father Hyder Ali did not hesitate to use their French-trained army against the Maharatta, Sira, Malabar, Coorg and Bednur kingdoms. He helped Hyder Ali defeat the British in the Second Mysore War, and negotiated the Treaty of Mangalore with them.

However, after the death of his father, Tipu Sultan was defeated in the Third and Fourth Anglo-Mysore War because of the combined forces of the English East India Company, the Nizam of Hyderabad, the Maratha Confederacy, and Travancore. Tipu Sultan's army could not defeat an enemy with such a vast militia. Tipu Sultan died defending his capital Srirangapattana, on 4 May 1799.

We all know or remember from high school texts that the first war of Indian Independence was the Sepoy mutiny which took place in 1857. However, Tipu Sultan's stand against the British dates back almost 60 years before the first recognised war of Indian independence. As a result of this strange omission from the annals of our Independence struggle, many questions arise in our minds. Why are Tipu Sultan's repeated stances not widely recognised by our own historians? How did the British manage to defeat him? As a ruler, why did Tipu Sultan have a problem with the British?

None of the other rulers who were his peers saw the British for what they were. They saw them as traders who were interested in taking India to the outside world (sounds similar to our current issues doesn't it? History surely does repeat itself!). How did this one man possess insight into what their real plans were?

If there is one thing that is a repeated fact when one reads about Tipu Sultan, it is that he was a great soldier. Was he that astute a statesman that he was able to see through British lies? Or was it because the British underestimated Tipu Sultan and treated him unfairly that he fought them? Before we delve deeper into the man and his legend, let us first examine the era in which he lived. It is said that to know a man, you must know his enemies. Let us talk a little about the British during the mid-18th century. Let us read about his father's life and his relationship with the British, and try to find Tipu Sultan's own history there.

Hyder Ali was the great-grandson of an Islamic fakir; his father was a chief constable at Budikote, near Kolar. Hyder Ali was born in Budikote between 1717 and 1722 and as a youth, Hyder Ali assisted his brother, a commander of a brigade in the Mysore Army. It was watching their skirmishes and tactics that helped Hyder Ali acquire a familiarity with the military tactics of the French. At this point, the French were under the leadership of Joseph François Dupleix (Governor General of the French establishment in India) who was the rival of Robert Clive.

At the siege of Devanhalli in 1749, Hyder Ali's prowess and astuteness in the military field and the fervour with which men fought under him did not go unnoticed. Nanjaraja, then the Raja of Mysore saw the potential in Hyder Ali and immediately gave him independent command over a section of the army.

During the next twelve years, Hyder Ali's energy and ability was repeatedly recognised by the Raja. Not only was Hyder Ali an expert warrior, he was also able to execute strategies and plan ahead based on enemy strength and weaknesses. He also possessed a mind that understood politics well and was keen on expanding his territory. Recognizing these as the primary goals of any ruler, Nanjaraja and the others realized that except officially, Hyder Ali was the ruler of the Mysore kingdom.

In 1763, during a war, the conquest of Kanara gave Hyder Ali possession of the treasures of Bednur (also spelt as Bednor). Astounded by what he saw, Hyder Ali resolved to make Bednur the most splendid capital in India, under his own name, and therefore he changed his name from Hyder Naik into Hyder Ali Khan Bahadur.

As part of the drive to make Bednur the finest capital in India, Hyder Ali waged many wars against neighbouring kingdoms to gain power over their lands and thereby increase his own wealth and expand his rule. By 1765, in the wars that he had waged successfully, he had defeated the Marathas and conquered Calicut.

At this time, the Madras Presidency (also known as Madras Province, it was a province of British India) began to feel threatened by the rising power of Hyder Ali. To curb this, in 1766 (Tipu Sultan would have been 16 years old at this point) it entered into an agreement with the Nizam of Hyderabad to furnish him with troops to be used against Hyder Ali. The Nizam of Hyderabad had as much reason to fear the rise of Hyder Ali. He felt that once Hyder Ali became sufficiently powerful, he was likely to attack Hyderabad and try to annex it into his own kingdom. Therefore the Nizam of Hyderabad too was distrustful of Hyder Ali and his plans of expansion.

The British Raj represented by the Madras Presidency thought it a wise move to befriend the enemy and enter into an alliance with it. They felt that this was the only way to diminish the threat of the common enemy, Hyder Ali. What the British Raj did not know was that at that point, the two native rulers has already been in contact with each other and had a plan of their own.

Hardly had this alliance between the Madras Presidency and Nizam of Hyderabad been formed than the secret arrangement between the two Indian powers was finalised. As a result of this, Colonel Smith's small force was met with a united army of 50,000 men and 100 guns.

This was a humiliating defeat for Colonel Smith's men. His own troops were defeated by the artillery and weapons provided to the Nizam in combination with the military superiority of Hyder Ali's men. This was the First Anglo-Mysore War and Colonel Smith's defeat at the Battle of Chengam (3 September 1767). Colonel Smith fought this joint alliance once more, and lost in Tiruvannamalai, which is now a district in present-day Tamil Nadu.

Upon the loss of his fleet and forts on the western coast during other battles in the First Anglo-Mysore War, Hyder Ali made overtures for peace to the British Raj. The Raj was functioning with up-to-date information, and the Madras Presidency knew that Hyder Ali's troops were diminished. As a result, they also knew that his bargaining power had significantly decreased.

The by-now overconfident Madras Presidency, though they recognised a worthy rival in Hyder Ali, made a huge mistake. They tried provoking him by rejecting his offer of peace. Through his experience in warfare and superior military tactics, he forced Colonel Smith to raise the siege of Bangalore, and brought his army within 5 miles of Madras. The British, realizing the folly that they had committed, and fearing yet another defeat and humiliation at his hands, signed the treaty of April 1769. A 19-year-old Tipu Sultan watched and understood the significance of this treaty!

This treaty was fairly simple and straightforward. It stated that the conquests made by both parties had to be restituted to rightful owners. The treaty also promised mutual aid and alliance in any defensive war that was engaged by either party which was not against each other.

This was followed by a commercial treaty in 1770 with the authorities of Bombay. This involved several trade agreements that were signed. This one allowed the British to bring their goods into the land, trade with the locals, and pay a certain percentage to the ruler, etc.

In 1772, during a war with the Marathas, Hyder Ali was defeated. Invoking the promise that was made in the treaty of 1769, Hyder Ali appealed to the British for assistance, but it was not provided to him. Tipu Sultan was 22 years old at this time; by then an able soldier and well versed in the craft of war and statesmanship. This breach of faith and treaty must have stung Hyder Ali but he got his revenge in 1778.

In 1778, the British declared war with France and resolved to drive the French out of India. Their mode of attacking the French was to capture Mahé, which was under French rule in 1779. In addition, they also annexed the lands of Hyder Ali's dependent and this gave Hyder Ali the pretext for the Second Anglo-Mysore War. He was finally able to avenge his honour by defeating the British and driving them out of his land. However, it was not that easy. It would take almost another 150 years and one iconic man before the British had had enough with India and granted her her freedom.

In the meantime, two more Anglo-Mysore Wars were fought before Tipu Sultan was defeated and killed. But now that we know how the story ends, let us rewind a little and start from Tipu Sultan's Childhood.

Tipu the Tiger

'It is far better to live like a Tiger for a day than to live like a jackal for a hundred years'. This maxim is often attributed to Tipu Sultan and has often been quoted to demonstrate his fervour, his bravery, and how he lived his life. The fact that he repeatedly fought the British and sought to drive the British out of his kingdom and out of India is a source of great pride for all Indians. That he did this before others could truly recognise the threat that the British posed is also another added bonus to those who love Tipu Sultan and his legend.

Though many historians still debate the exact date, it is widely agreed that Tipu Sultan was born on 10

November 1750 (Friday, 10th Zil-Hijja, 1163 AH). His father was Hyder Ali and his mother was Fatima or Fakhr-un-nissa, daughter of Shahal Tharique, the governor of the fort of Cuddapah.

Let us skip a little ahead to get a description of the adult Tipu Sultan. Alexander Beatson published a volume entitled "View of the Origin and Conduct of the War with the late Tippoo Sultan" described Tipu Sultan thus: "His stature was about five feet eight inches; he had a short neck, square shoulders, and was rather corpulent: his limbs were small, particularly his feet and hands; he had large full eyes, small arched eyebrows, and an aquiline nose; his complexion was fair, and the general expression of his countenance, not void of dignity".

We now return to his youth where Tipu Sultan exhibited a keen mind that was able to absorb facts quickly, and was a talented linguist. Tipu Sultan was able to pick up several languages and speak them fluently. He was also very interested in religion. A religious man himself, Tipu practised the Sunni branch of Islam. He was keen on becoming a Sufi but his father Hyder Ali insisted that he become a capable soldier and from there, it was only a few steps for Tipu Sultan to become a great leader.

Perhaps it was this interest in the mystic traditions of Islam that allowed Tipu Sultan to be tolerant towards all religions. His treatment of his Hindu subjects is highly disputed where one branch of History devoutly states that he massacred many Hindus. We shall discuss more of that later. However, another theory persists that through this carnage Tipu Sultan was a highly tolerant man. They also believe that he was a humanist who believed in the rights of all to coexist peacefully in his country. It was under his guidance and patronage that many Hindu temples were well preserved. His building of the first church also shows his magnanimity, and his treatment of his British captives speaks volumes about his true nature outside of the battlefield.

We will discuss more of Tipu's rule and his farsightedness that allowed him to develop Mysore during times of peace. We shall also take a peek into his diplomatic ability after we discuss his illustrious military career which spanned almost his entire life, with him actively participating in war when he was as young as 15!

Tipu Sultan's Early Military Career

Upon instructions from Hyder Ali, Tipu Sultan was instructed in military tactics by French officers in Hyder Ali's employment. Tipu Sultan was present in Hyder Ali's negotiations with the Nizam of Hyderabad in the First Mysore War. In fact, according to historians, it was Tipu Sultan's tact and resourcefulness that impressed the Nizam and won him over to Hyder Ali's side.

It was Tipu Sultan who obtained the sanction of the Treaty of Alliance between the Nizam of Hyderabad and Hyder Ali in 1767. Tipu Sultan was sent to the Nizam's Camp as the head of 6000 troops and he successfully concluded the treaty. This was the first diplomatic assignment that Tipu Sultan was sent on by Hyder Ali. During the rest of the First Anglo-Mysore War and during the Second Anglo-Mysore War before Hyder Ali died, Tipu Sultan would not only command several troops, but he would go on several such diplomatic missions.

It must have been this training he received that aided him thereafter. It is a widely acknowledged fact that Tipu Sultan's aides were spread throughout the world and his ability to strike trade with many countries was primarily due to his diplomatic abilities.

Coming back to the First Anglo-Mysore War, Tipu Sultan was well received by the Nizam of Hyderabad, who conferred on him the title of "Nasib-ud-daula" (Fortune of the State) and also "Fateh Ali Khan". At 15, he accompanied his father Hyder Ali against the British in the First Mysore War in 1766. He commanded a corps of cavalry in the invasion of the Carnatic in 1767 at age 16.

After the death of Peshwa Madhava Rao in 1772, he was sent to the northern part of Mysore to recover the territories which the Marathas had occupied. By the time of Second Mysore War he had gained great experience both of warfare and diplomacy. He also distinguished himself in the First Anglo-Maratha War of 1775–1779.

It was not just the coaching that he received from excellent warriors that distinguished Tipu Sultan from every other hero, but also his innate knack for war. Like Hyder Ali, just through keen observation, Tipu Sultan was able to become a great warrior. He was equally skilled at strategising and attacking but he also possessed the ability to inspire his men to follow him anywhere, even to death.

It is truly the mark of a great hero and warrior that men knew that they were going to their deaths but still fought valiantly and with honour. Men such as Alexander, Napoleon and Tipu Sultan were few and far between, but their presence illuminated a bloody saga with their tales of inspiration and valour.

The First Mysore War has already been discussed but a brief recap is provided here. Hyder Ali's expansion was noticed by the British Government who decided to enter into an alliance with the Nizam of Hyderabad. Betraying the confidence of the British, the Nizam and Hyder Ali along with Tipu Sultan who was a lad of merely 15 years of age, attacked and defeated Colonel Smith and his army with 50,000 men and 100 guns. Later in the same war, a lad of merely 17 years, Tipu Sultan made such a surprising dash on Madras in 1767, that the entire English Council, who were all members of the Madras Government, sought refuge in a ship.

It was during this almost-three-year war (the First Anglo-Mysore War raged between 1766-1769) that Hyder Ali's fleet and forts along the Western Coast were destroyed and led him to appeal for peace. Tipu Sultan witnessed the British refuse Hyder Ali's offer for peace and in turn, suffer for it as Hyder Ali possessed a disciplined military and superior warfare technique. The British were thus forced to sign the treaty of April 1769.

It was breach of this treaty that led to the Second Anglo-Mysore War (1780-1784). A breach of faith and treaty by the British during an earlier war against the Marathas (in 1772, already discussed earlier) forced Hyder Ali to commit himself to a French alliance. When the French declared war against Britain in 1778, the British (then firmly entrenched in Madras) resolved to drive the French out of India by taking the few enclaves of French possessions left on the subcontinent.

As part of this drive, the British captured Mahé on the Malabar coast in 1779, and annexed certain lands belonging to a dependent of Hyder Ali. It was then that Hyder Ali and Tipu Sultan engaged in the Second Mysore War.

The Battle of Pollilur which took place in 1780 near the city of Kanchipuram was a part of the second Anglo-Mysore War. Tipu Sultan was dispatched by Hyder Ali with 10,000 men and 18 guns to intercept Colonel Baillie who was on his way to join Sir Hector Munro. Out of 360 Europeans in the fleet, about 200 were captured alive, and the sepoys, about 3800 in number, suffered very high casualties.

Sir Hector Munro was the victor of the Battle of Buxar. He had earlier defeated three Indian rulers (the Mughal emperor Shah Alam, the Nawab of Oudh Shuja-ud-daula, and the Nawab of Bengal Mir Qasim). He was forced to retreat to Madras, abandoning his artillery in the tank of Kanchipuram. There are many accounts of this ignominious retreat and some of them are exaggerated tales to highlight Tipu Sultan's valour. Though the exact details may be distorted for creative purposes, the fact that Tipu Sultan was able to orchestrate such fear is something every Indian is to be proud of.

In December 1781 Tipu Sultan had successfully seized Chittur from the British. He fell with such fury on Colonel Bailey in 1782, that the entire English army was either cut or taken prisoners. Colonel Bailey himself languished for long in the prisons of Srirangapatna.

In February 1782, Tipu Sultan, leading a large body of troops, defeated Colonel Braithwaite on the banks of the Kollidam. The British army, consisting of 100 Europeans, 300 cavalry, 1400 sepoys and 10 field pieces, was the standard size of the colonial armies. Tipu Sultan had seized all the guns and taken the entire detachment prisoners. Colonel Braithwaite was kept as a captive for long in Srirangapatna.

Although the British were defeated during the Second Mysore War, Tipu Sultan realized that the British were a new kind of threat in India. On becoming the Sultan at the death of his father later that year (Hyder Ali died in December 1782), he worked to check the advances of the British by making alliances with the Marathas and Mughals. The Second Mysore War came to an end with the Treaty of Mangalore signed in 1784. It was the last occasion when an Indian king dictated terms to the British, and as a result of that, the treaty is a prestigious document in the history of India.

Warren Hastings, the first Governor-General of India, called the Mangalore Treaty a humiliating pacification. He appealed to the King and Parliament to punish the Madras Government, for "the faith and honour of the British nation have been equally violated." Warren Hastings wholly blamed the Madras Presidency for not warning the Government of the threat that Hyder

Ali and his son Tipu Sultan posed earlier. In addition to the ignorance that they had forced upon the British Government, an added insult was that they had underestimated the diplomatic abilities of both father and son. A direct result of this gross underestimation was that the British had been beaten using their own weapons and artillery.

The British worked hard from that day, 11 March 1784, to subvert Tipu Sultan's power. However, the Mangalore Treaty was a testament to the diplomatic skill of Tipu Sultan. He had honourably concluded a long-drawn war. He frustrated the Maratha designs to seize his northern possessions. The even greater advantage was the psychological impact of his victory with the British, because the mode of conclusion was highly satisfactory to him. He called the shots on when the war would end, and he knew that it was a greater victory than the one won on a battlefield.

The march of the Commissioner all the way from Madras to Mangalore seeking peace made Munro remark that such indignities were showered on the British "that limited efforts seemed necessary to repudiate the Treaty at the earliest time." Public opinion in the country highly gratified Tipu Sultan, who felt it was his great triumph over the British. That was the only bright spot in his contest with the

British, his proud event in which he had humbled a mighty power.

Under Tipu Sultan's leadership the Mysore army became a model and a school of military science to Indian powers. Before we discuss the other two Anglo-Mysore Wars which ended up sapping the life of Tipu Sultan, let us digress for a few moments and talk about Tipu Sultan the ruler.

Tipu Sultan the Farsighted Ruler

"Agriculture is the life-blood of the nation. This land, rich and fertile, will reward those that work on it. Famine and want are either the result of sloth and ignorance or of corruption" (Tipu's circular to all Amildars, 1788).

Despite his hectic political and military involvement, Tipu Sultan never ignored his main task of improving the life and conditions of his people. He understood that while wars were essential to ensure the security of his nation, it was his work to improve the living condition of his subjects. As a result, he was very involved in the improvement of agriculture and industry. He promoted trade and commerce. His novel system of administration of justice (which we will study in detail later), his concept of a navy, his opening of factories, and his despatch of embassies to distant lands, linked the small State of Mysore with the bigger world. All this marked him as a better ruler.

During his rule, Tipu Sultan was always keen on looking into the future and bettering his kingdom. He was busy not only with strategising against the British but also in ensuring that his Mysore would for long remain an example to other cities across the country. He laid the foundation for a dam, where the famous Krishna Raja Sagara Dam across the river Cauvery was later built. He also completed the project of Lal Bagh started by his father Hyder Ali, and built roads, public buildings, and ports along the Kerala shoreline.

An astute diplomat, he recognized the need to expand his borders not just through annexing lands but also through trade. His trade extended to countries which included Sri Lanka, Afghanistan, France, Turkey, and Iran. It would not be a stretch to assume that it was through these trade ties that Tipu Sultan was able to garner a better view of the world and what the British truly had in store for India.

Always a warrior, his leadership made the Mysore army a school of military science to Indian princes.

His superior skills in formations and his keen understanding of battle made him an encyclopaedic source on strategy and the art of war.

Dr. A.P.J. Abdul Kalam, the former President of India, in his Tipu Sultan Shaheed Memorial Lecture in Bangalore (30 November 1991), called Tipu Sultan the "innovator of the world's first war rocket". Two of the rockets that were deployed by Tipu Sultan against the British were captured by the British at Srirangapatna and are displayed in the Woolwich Museum Artillery in London.

In his military career, most of Tipu Sultan's campaigns resulted in remarkable successes. He managed to subdue all the petty kingdoms in the south. He defeated the Marathas and the Nizams several times and was also one of the few Indian rulers to have defeated British armies. He is also said to have started a new coinage system, banking system, a new calendar, and a new system of weights and measures.

The Nitty Gritties of Tipu Sultan's Rule

Tipu Sultan's system of administration was far ahead of its times. He recognised the value of trade and impressed upon his cabinet of ministers to find new avenues and identify new opportunities of trade. Therefore his administration not only concentrated on the farmer and how well to maximise his potential, it was also an astute watcher of the then business world.

His ministers and excellent network of spies were always briefing Tipu Sultan on the goings on of the world. With his hand firmly on the pulse of the world, Tipu Sultan was able to transform the sleepy town of Mysore into a bustling industrial arena.

To remove economic disparities that existed during his time, Tipu Sultan undertook various commercial measures. He devised a plan of state capitalism. His commercial regulations created a scheme of banking organisation in which small investors received higher benefits. It was a pioneering experiment of a type of cooperative bank which encouraged small savings.

To strengthen this banking system Tipu Sultan launched the state control of trade, commerce and industries. Mysore was rich in commercial crops such as silk, sandalwood, pepper, cardamom, coconut, elephants, and ivory which were in great demand in the Western market. Tipu was keen that the trade of these commodities should not fall into foreign hands.

Therefore, the state itself became the greatest exporter and importer of goods, which were sent out, and brought in, by his fleet of merchant ships. The hold of private bankers, money lenders and middle-men was vastly reduced. It was not just trade and commerce, but also arts and crafts that attracted his attention for state control.

A large number of workshops were set up, which manufactured guns, muskets, glass, cannon, paper, cutlery, cloth, sugar, and a host of other articles. It was his dream to keep Mysore in the vanguard of the ship-building industry. He built a navy both for commerce and war. In 1793, he ordered 100 ships to be built, all with indigenous material. He paid attention to the manufacture of arms and ammunition. The factory at Srirangapattna converted iron into steel, and manufactured armaments. He named his iron-works as Taramandals, which were four in number, at Srirangapatna, Bangalore, Chitradurga and Bednur. A machine was devised which bored cannon with power generated by the flow of water.

In the midst of the war against the Marathas and the Nizam, he issued instructions to take care of the silk worms which were being brought from Bengal. Sericulture received great attention under his rule. It is said that he was so fond of horticulture and gardening that all his correspondence with foreign dignitaries would invariably carry a request for new varieties of seeds and plants.

He changed the land tenure, which entitled the cultivators to own the land. He gave wasteland free of rent for cultivation. He put an end to the farming of the land to the highest bidder, and appointment of revenue officers for collecting revenue. He abolished the grant of "jagirs". He introduced "takavi" loans which helped the peasants in lean seasons. The existing forced labour was done away with. To discourage needless litigation, he encouraged the villagers to settle disputes among themselves.

His love of plants was so great that he hit upon a novel idea of dispensing justice. For various offences committed by the people, he fixed proportionate punishment. His brand of justice did not deal with imposing fines or jailing someone, but it made the criminal plant trees. According to Tipu Sultan's new system of justice, once found guilty and sentenced with growing plants, they needed to water them, and bring them up to a particular height.

His social reforms included the prohibition of liquor. He put an end to the purchase and sale of abandoned girls and children. He discouraged the use of tobacco. He checked lavish expenditure on the celebration of weddings and brought about other social reforms. His sense of justice can be deduced from the fact that he punished his eldest son, Fateh Haider, for taking vegetables without the permission of the owner.

He thought of setting up a university at Srirangapatna and even named it Jami-al-Umur. He started the first newspaper, Fauji Akhbar. He was an author and knew Urdu, Persian Arabic, Kannada, Marathi, English and

French. More than 45 books were written during his reign. His library consisted of 2000 manuscripts, one of them being the handwritten Quran by Aurangazeb. He also commissioned a massive album that depicted the pictures of all great Sufi saints both of India and abroad.

He was also an astute businessman and he searched high and low and secured artisans who would make him guns, muskets and a host of other weaponry. His attention to detail in warfare-related commodities was probably where his love for innovation began.

Tipu Sultan had an inquisitive mind and while most of it was spent on checking the advances of the British, his love for innovation and improvement of what already existed was high. His palace is said to have many such trinkets that he commissioned artisans to make for his amusement and study.

Alexander Beatson who wrote about Tipu Sultan mentions that he was "passionately fond of new inventions. In his palace was found a great variety of curious swords, daggers, fusils, pistols, and blunderbusses; some were of exquisite workmanship, mounted with gold, or silver, and beautifully inlaid and ornamented with tigers' heads and stripes, or with Persian and Arabic verses".

Out of these, the one that is most indicative of the martial nature of Tipu Sultan and that also betrays his sense of humour is Tipu's Tiger. This was an automaton representing a tiger attacking a European soldier, made for Tipu Sultan. It is now on display at the Victoria and Albert Museum, London.

Tipu however had certain priorities; freedom of the land topped the list. Any sacrifice was too small for its protection. Therefore, he diverted the resources of his state first to preserve and protect freedom. Manufacture of armaments was imperative, without which neither he nor his state could survive.

It was Tipu who assessed the trends of Western political and economic development, which aimed at subverting Indian economy to suit colonial interests. Instead of succumbing to foreign forces, Tipu attempted to present an alternative model, which was his own brain-child. It was a novel idea and had there been an opportunity for it to have been implemented, it would have yielded good results.

This model was to be evolved by transferring western mercantilism on to the structure of Indian economy. Not only would this involve following the western system of trade, it would also eliminate the harmful effects of indigenous feudalism. By abolishing the

Zamindari system and by promoting trade, this new model was expected to push to the growth of Indian capitalism.

It was in the sphere of economic polices and measures that Tipu Sultan's role was unique among all the Indian rulers. He went for a substantive change in all aspects of economy, whether agriculture, trade or industry.

Tipu Sultan – a Villain or a Magnanimous Ruler?

As a devout Muslim ruler in a largely Hindu land, Tipu Sultan's religious legacy has now become a source of religious and historical controversy. As mentioned earlier, two streams of thought exist; in one, a large number of groups proclaim him a great warrior for the faith, while there are groups who revile him as a bigot who massacred Hindus.

It is not surprising that Tipu Sultan faced problems in establishing the legitimacy of his rule. He was torn between reconciling his desire to be seen as a devout Islamic ruler and the need to be pragmatic. It was necessary for Tipu Sultan to avoid antagonising the majority of his subjects who happened to be Hindus.

Tipu Sultan has often been criticized as being anti-Hindu. Some historians claim that he had a repressive attitude towards Hindus and was harsh towards them. It is widely accepted that in the early part of his reign, he appears to have been notably more aggressive and more religiously doctrinaire than his father, Hyder Ali. C. K. Kareem, a noted historian points out that Tipu Sultan issued an edict for the destruction of Hindu temples in Kerala. He is alleged to have ordered massacres and forced conversion of Brahmins in Kerala.

A lore exists that Tipu Sultan slew between 500 to 800 relatives of the Tirumaliengar as retaliation because he found out that Tirumaliengar, on behalf of the dowager queen Rani Lakshammanni of Mysore, had entered into an agreement with the British in 1790. During this period, furious of this betrayal, Tipu Sultan also ordered that Shamaiya Iyengar be blinded. Shamaiya Iyengar was one of the ministers during the time of Hyder Ali and was also minister for communication [posts] and police during Tipu Sultan's time.

However, it is also said that Tipu Sultan forgave Shamaiya when his son fought against the English during the last Anglo-Mysore War and died due to a gunshot in the chest. As a result of the massacre of the Hindu relatives, it is said that Mandyam Iyengars, particularly of the Bharadwaja Gotra, do not celebrate Naraka Chaturdashi during Deepawali.

On an aside, why should this incident be blown out of its context? If he had slayed 800 Muslims for betrayal of the nation's interests and for entering into an agreement with the enemy, would it have been alright?

This incident or slaughter as it has been portrayed does not in any way indicate the partisan tendencies of Tipu Sultan. It only highlights that he was a furious patriot and whenever he saw a move that undermined his efforts to drive the British out of the country, he retaliated in a forceful way.

Having said this, it should also be examined as to who wrote these accounts of Tipu Sultan's brutality. Many in the current crop of historians argue that stories of Tipu Sultan's religious persecution of Hindus and Christians are largely derived from the work of early British authors such as Kirkpatrick and Wilks, whom they do not consider to be entirely reliable. These early British authors had strong vested interests in presenting Tipu Sultan as a tyrant from whom the British had "liberated" Mysore. In fact, both Wilks and Kirkpatrick had taken part in the wars against Tipu

Sultan and were closely connected to the administrations of Lord Cornwallis and Richard Wellesley. The nature of truth seems elusive in an even more obvious light when Muslim accounts of conversions arise.

The English versions of what happened were intended to malign Tipu Sultan, and to be used as propaganda against him. However, Muslim accounts such as Kirmani's "Nishan-e Haidari" are also unreliable; in their anxiety to represent the Sultan as a champion of Islam, they had a tendency to exaggerate and distort the facts: Kirmani claims that 70,000 Coorgis were converted, when forty years later the entire population of Coorg was still less than that number. According to Ramchandra Rao "Punganuri", the true number of converts was estimated at only about 500.

The portrayal of Tipu Sultan as a religious bigot is disputed, and some sources suggest that he in fact often embraced religious pluralism. An example of this was the diverseness present in his cabinet. Tipu Sultan's treasurer was Krishna Rao, Shamaiya Iyengar was his Minister of Post and Police, his brother Ranga Iyengar was an officer, and Purnaiya held the very important post of "Mir Asaf". Moolchand and Sujan Rai were his chief agents at the Mughal court, and his chief "Peshkar", Suba Rao, was also a Hindu.

There is also such evidence as grant deeds, and correspondence between his court and temples. However, there are those who say that his having donated jewellery and documented land grants to several temples was because he was compelled to do so in order to make alliances with Hindu rulers. However, records indicate that between 1782 and 1799, Tipu Sultan issued 34 "Sanads" (deeds) of endowment to temples in his domain, while also presenting many of them with gifts of silver and gold plates.

In 1791, Maratha horsemen under Raghunath Rao Patwardhan raided the temple and monastery of Sringeri Shankaracharya, killing and wounding many, and plundering the monastery of all its valuable possessions. The incumbent Shankaracharya petitioned Tipu Sultan for help.

A bunch of about 30 letters written in Kannada, which were exchanged between Tipu Sultan's court and the Sringeri Shankaracharya were discovered in 1916 by the Director of Archaeology in Mysore. Tipu Sultan expressed his indignation and grief at the news of the raid, and wrote:

"People who have sinned against such a holy place are sure to suffer the consequences of their misdeeds at no distant date in this Kali age in accordance with the verse: "Hasadbhih kriyate karma ruladbhir-anubhuyate" (People do [evil] deeds smilingly but suffer the consequences crying)." He immediately ordered the "Asaf" of Bednur to supply the Swami with 200 "rahatis" (fanams) in cash and other gifts and articles. Tipu Sultan's interest in the Sringeri temple continued for many years, and he was still writing to the Swami in the 1790s CE.

In light of this and other events, Tipu Sultan has often been described as a defender of the Hindu Dharma, who also patronized other temples including one at Melkote, for which he issued a Kannada decree that the Shrivaishnava invocatory verses there should be recited in the traditional form.

The temple at Melkote still has gold and silver vessels with inscriptions indicating that they were presented by the Sultan. Tipu Sultan also presented four silver cups to the Lakshmikanta Temple at Kalale.

Tipu Sultan does seem to have repossessed unauthorised grants of land made to Brahmins and temples. But closer examination of this act shows that those which had proper "sanads" were not repossessed by the Sultan. It was a normal practice for any ruler, Muslim or Hindu, to reposess unauthorised land on his accession or on the conquest of new territory.

However, his generosity was also boundless. The Srikanteswara temple at Nanjungud was presented with a jewelled cup and some precious stones. To another temple, Nanjundeswara, in the same town of Nanjungud, he gave a greenish linga. To the Ranganatha temple at Srirangapatana he gifted seven silver cups and a silver camphor burner. This temple was hardly a stone's throw from his palace from where he would listen with equal respect the ringing of temple bells, and the Muezzin's call from the mosque.

Another instance of establishing what an enlightened ruler Tipu Sultan was is his desire for the humane treatment of his prisoners. In fact, there existed a clause in the proposed treaty of alliance with the French which stated, "I demand that male and female prisoners as well English and Portuguese, who shall be taken by the republican troops or by mine, shall be treated with humanity, and with regard to their persons, that they shall be transported at our joint expense out of India to some place far distant from the territories of the allies."

However, in the interest of truth, it should also be mentioned that during the storming of Srirangapattana by the British in 1799, thirteen murdered British prisoners were discovered; they had been killed by either having their necks broken or nails driven into their skulls.

Tipu Sultan was also a founder-member of the Jacobin Club. This club was the largest and most powerful political club of the French Revolution. To this day, the terms Jacobin and Jacobinism are used as pejoratives (pejorative is a term that is generally a derogatory label) for left-wing revolutionary politics.

While accepting the membership, he said of France, "Behold my acknowledgement of the standard of your country, which is dear to me, and to which I am allied; it shall always be supported in my country, as it has been in the Republic, my sister!". He was named as Citizen Tipu Sultan.

Tipu Sultan the Diplomat

Turkey in the 18th Century was still a force to reckon with. She had resisted Russian expansion and had held vast territories in Eastern Europe. Tipu viewed the expansion of the British as a threat to the entire Islamic world and called the English "the enemies of the faith".

He desired the Turkish Sultan to lead a crusade against the Europeans. For this purpose Tipu sent an Embassy to Constantinople in 1784 under Usman Khan. The response of this machine being favourable, he sent an enlarged embassy of four persons in 1785.

The purpose was to conclude a political and military treaty against the English. In his letter to Sultan Abdul Hameed, Tipu wrote about the excesses the British had committed in India and sought military support. The fourth article of the proposed treaty spoke of military co-operation between Mysore and Turkey. This Treaty had five clauses, one of which referred to trade facilities in Basra in exchange for similar facilities in Mysore.

Yet another clause stipulated that Turkey was to spare as many technicians as possible to assist Tipu in gun and cannon-making. Tipu said that the neglect of commerce and industry was the main cause of the decline in the East.

The envoys were treated with great courtesy in Constantinople, but the main issue of the treaty was evaded. Sultan Abdul Hameed said that the Russians had set their eyes on the Ottoman Empire, and he was engaged in resisting their menace.

The British had shrewdly exploited this weakness of Turkey to keep it on their side, and the Turks would not alienate the English at a time when Russia was at their door. The ambassadors returned to India empty-handed.

However Tipu had very close relations with France. He was very hopeful of their support, for their historic role in the American war of Independence had removed the English from their thirteen rich colonies in the new world. Moreover, Tipu was aware of fact that the British were building up their empire in India by making one prince fight against the other.

This aspect of the western technique of divide and rule had an echo in Tipu in his efforts to woo the French, who were the traditional rivals of the English. The Anglo-French animosity went back to the days of Crecy and Agricourt, and it lasted all through the centuries until the First World War of 1914.

Thus the bitter opposition to the British was a common cause between the French and Tipu, and he regarded them as his natural allies. Just as the English were making the Indians fight against the Indians, Tipu too would make the Europeans fight against the Europeans. There were certain definite advantages in such a policy, as the Indians would get a respite. According to Tipu Sultan, both western powers would get exhausted, seek Indian support, and in the confusion either of the two European powers would be eliminated. If the English were to be eliminated, it would be better for India, for greater danger seemed to lurk from them.

Tipu was also aware that in the struggle for supremacy, the Dutch had eliminated the Portuguese, and the English had eliminated the Dutch from India, but the French and English were still present. The French were not as weak as the Portuguese, or the Dutch, and their support had proved decisive in the new world.

The constant presence of a French regiment in his army, their influence at his court, their consistent support to Mysore since Hyder Ali's days, and a frequent visit of French adventurers to his capital, raised Tipu Sultan's hopes that the drama of American War of Independence could be repeated in India.

The Third and Fourth Anglo-Mysore Wars

While Tipu Sultan organised embassies to foreign lands and improved agriculture in Mysore, his enemies were plotting. It was dangerous times before the Third and Fourth Anglo-Mysore Wars.

The Treaty of Mangalore that was signed at the end of the Second Mysore War carried the seeds of strife with the Marathas. They were disappointed because they had expected a recovery of their lost territories as payment for being mediators. Instead, Tipu Sultan emerged as a victor and even the British could not humble him with their increased military strength. This incited the jealousy of both the Marathas and the

Nizam of Hyderabad who fought a war with him for two years from 1785 to 1787.

The Nizam of Hyderabad was not friendly towards Mysore ever since he came to power in 1761. He regarded himself as the overlord of the entire south, and expected Hyder Ali and Tipu Sultan to be his dependants. Since the Nizam of Hyderabad was not as proficient in warfare and did not possess the keen military insight that the father-son duo possessed, he allied himself either with the Marathas or the English to distress the Mysore rulers. There was always a pro-British party at Hyderabad which dissuaded the Nizam of Hyderabad from being cordial with Tipu Sultan.

Despite the alliance of the Marathas and the Nizam of Hyderabad, Tipu had the upper hand. The war came to an end in April 1787 with the signing of the Treaty of Gajendragadh. Tipu Sultan ceded Badami to the Marathas hoping to win their support against the English or at the very least, to prevent them from joining with the English. But Tipu was disappointed in his expectations. Far from joining him to remove the English from India, the Marathas and the Nizam of Hyderabad joined the English in a powerful confederacy against Tipu in the Third Mysore War.

The allies struggled hard for nearly two years from 1790 to 1792. Lord Cornwallis assumed command

and with great difficulty was successful, in a surprise night-attack, in entering into the island of Srirangapatna on 6th Feb. 1792. Tipu was forced to make peace by surrendering half of his kingdom, paying three crore rupees as indemnity, and sending his two sons as hostages to Madras. This was a serious blow to Tipu.

However, Tipu Sultan was soon able to build his power again. He paid the indemnity and got his sons back. He intensified his contacts with the French, the Turks and the Afghans. The Nizam of Hyderabad was also convinced, and he rejoined the alliance. The Nizam of Hyderabad recruited a contingent of 1400 troops under Raymond, who was friendly to Tipu. Napoleon was on his way to join Tipu.

Zaman Shah of Afghanistan was also willing to join the fight to remove the British from India. When all these plans were about to mature, fate intervened. Napoleon was defeated at Accre in Syria and forced back to France. Zaman Shah was made to beat a hasty retreat to Kabul because of British machinations that brought about a rear action from Iran on Afghanistan.

Arthur Wellesly forced the Nizam of Hyderabad to disband Raymond and accept a British detachment under subsidiary systems. Having finished this task, Lord Wellesley declared war on Tipu and sent the largest British army ever assembled in India. Three armies, one from Bombay, and two British (one of which included Arthur Wellesley), marched into Mysore in 1799 and besieged the capital Srirangapatnam in the Fourth Mysore War.

There were over 26,000 soldiers of the British East India Company comprising about 4000 Europeans, the rest being Indians. A column was supplied by the Nizam of Hyderabad consisting of ten battalions and over 16,000 cavalry, and many soldiers were sent by the Marathas. Thus the soldiers in the British force numbered over 50,000 soldiers whereas Tipu Sultan had only about 30,000.

The Fourth Mysore War was a short affair. Keeping Tipu in false hopes, he suddenly surprised him by unacceptable demands. When Tipu refused to accept them, the English breached the fort and in a bloody encounter, fighting against heavy odds, he was killed on 4 May 1799. The hope for the freedom of the land through Tipu Sultan's relentless fight was thus extinguished. He died a soldier's death for the defence of the cherished values of land under the spontaneous combustion of hostile forces.

Let us stop for a moment and pay homage to the keen innovator and warrior in Tipu Sultan by studying his artillery.

Tipu's Advanced Weaponry

A military tactic developed by Tipu Sultan and his father Hyder Ali, was mass attacks of infantry formations with the use of rocket brigades. In fact, Tipu Sultan wrote a military manual called Fathul Mujahidin in which 200 rocket-men were prescribed to each Mysorean "cushoon" (brigade).

Mysore had 16 to 24 cushoons of infantry. The areas of town where rockets and fireworks were manufactured were known as Taramandal Pet ("Galaxy Market").

The rocket-men were trained to launch their rockets at an angle calculated from the diameter of the cylinder and the distance of the target. In addition, wheeled rocket launchers capable of launching five to ten rockets almost simultaneously were used in war.

The rockets could be of various sizes, but usually consisted of a tube of soft hammered iron about 8" long and 1½ - 3" diameter, closed at one end and strapped to a shaft of bamboo about 4ft. long. The iron tube acted as a combustion chamber and contained well-packed black powder propellant. A rocket carrying about one pound of powder could travel almost 1,000 yards. In contrast, rockets in Europe not being iron cased, could not take large chamber pressures and as a consequence, were not capable of reaching distances anywhere near that.

Hyder Ali's father, the Naik or chief constable at Budikote, commanded 50 rocket-men for the Nawab of Arcot. There was a regular Rocket Corps in the Mysore Army, beginning with about 1200 men in Hyder Ali's time.

At the Battle of Pollilur (1780), during the Second Anglo-Mysore War, Colonel William Braille's ammunition stores were thought to have been detonated by a hit from one of Haidar Ali's Mysore rockets resulting in a humiliating British defeat.

In the Third Anglo-Mysore War of 1792, there is mention of two rocket units fielded by Tipu Sultan, 120 men and 131 men respectively. Lt. Col. Knox was attacked by rockets near Srirangapatna on the night of 6 February 1792, while advancing towards the Kaveri River from the north. The Rocket Corps ultimately reached a strength of about 5000 in Tipu Sultan's army.

Mysore rockets were also used for ceremonial purposes. When the Jacobin Club of Mysore sent a delegation to Tipu Sultan, 500 rockets were launched as part of the gun salute. During the Fourth Anglo-Mysore War, rockets were again used on several occasions. One of these involved Colonel Arthur Wellesley. Arthur Wellesley was defeated by Tipu's Diwan, Purnaiya, at the Battle of Sultanpet Tope. Quoting Forrest, "At this point (near the village of Sultanpet, Figure 5) there was a large tope, or grove, which gave shelter to Tipu's rocket-men, and had to be cleaned out before the siege could be pressed closer to Srirangapattana Island. The commander chosen for this operation was Col. Wellesley, but advancing towards the tope after dark on the 5 April 1799, he was set upon with rockets and musket-fires, lost his way and, as Beatson politely puts it, had to "postpone the attack" until a more favourable opportunity should offer.

The following day, Wellesley launched a fresh attack with a larger force, and took the whole position without losing a single man. On 22 April 1799, twelve days before the main battle, rocketeers worked their way around to the rear of the British encampment, then 'threw a great number of rockets at the same instant' to signal the beginning of an assault by 6,000 Indian infantry and a corps of Frenchmen, all directed by Mir Golam Hussain and Mohomed Hulleen Mir Mirans.

The rockets burst into the air like shells. Others, called ground rockets, on striking the ground, would rise again and bound along in a serpentine motion until their force was spent. According to one British observer, a young English officer named Bayly: "So pestered were we with the rocket boys that there was no moving without danger from the destructive missiles". He continued: "The rockets and musketry from 20,000 of the enemy were incessant. No hail could be thicker. Every illumination of blue lights was accompanied by a shower of rockets, some of which entered the head of the column, passing through to the rear, causing death, wounds, and dreadful lacerations from the long bamboos of twenty or thirty feet, which are invariably attached to them."

During the conclusive British attack on Srirangapattana on May 2, 1799, a British shot struck a magazine of rockets within Tipu Sultan's fort, causing it to explode and send a towering cloud of black smoke, with cascades of exploding white light rising up from the battlements.

On the afternoon of 4 May when the final attack on the fort was led by Baird, he was again met by "furious musket and rocket fire", but this did not help much; in about an hour's time the Fort was taken; perhaps in another hour Tipu had been shot (the precise time of his death is not known), and the war was effectively over.

After the fall of Srirangapattana, 600 launchers, 700 serviceable rockets and 9,000 empty rockets were found. Some of the rockets had pierced cylinders, to allow them to act like incendiaries, while some had iron points or steel blades bound to the bamboo. By attaching these blades to rockets they became very unstable towards the end of their flight causing the blades to spin around like flying scythes, cutting down all in their path.

These experiences eventually led to the Royal Woolwich Arsenal's beginning a military rocket R&D program in 1801, their first demonstration of solid-fuel rockets in 1805, and publication of 'A Concise Account of the Origin and Progress of the Rocket

Tipu's tomb

System' in 1807 by William Congreve, son of the arsenal's commandant.

Congreve rockets were soon systematically used by the British during the Napoleonic Wars and their confrontation with the US during 1812–14. These descendants of Mysore rockets even find mention in the Star Spangled Banner, the American National Anthem.

The End of Tipu and the Very First Resistance

In 1780 CE he declared himself to be the Padishah or Emperor of Mysore, and struck coinage in his own name without reference to the reigning Mughal Emperor Shah Alam II.

In his correspondence with other Islamic rulers such as Shah Zaman of Afghanistan, Tipu Sultan used this title and declared that he intended to establish an Islamic Empire in the entire country, along the lines of the Mughal Empire. At this point, it is important to note that the Mughal Empire was at its nadir during this period. His alliance with the French was supposedly aimed at achieving this goal by driving his main rivals, the British, out of the subcontinent.

Tipu Sultan's entire life was devoted to war and stopping the British from gaining control over his kingdom. In between the many wars that he fought, he always found time for his people. Tipu Sultan never forgot that his people depended on him to improve their lives. They looked towards him for guidance. He always behaved in the most appropriate and responsible manner.

Tipu even instituted social reforms to improve the life of his people. He created a new system of generating revenue for his kingdom. He tried to create an alternative model of governing. He studied the Western style of trade and tried to implement it here. He exported all that Mysore had to offer and imported anything he felt Mysore needed. He was careful about the welfare of his subjects and ensured their safety and security at all times. Because he was first and foremost a splendid warrior, he also ensured that his army was well equipped with the best guns. He also bolstered his strength by commissioning a navy to support his troops. When all these are stacked together, it is therefore easy to forget that Tipu Sultan also had a religious side and was a kind and generous man who was keen on learning, innovation and religion.

Tipu Sultan lived and died a Hero. He will always be remembered as the Tiger that bravely stood against the British, dared oppose them repeatedly, and gave them nightmares. Tipu Sultan lives in the heart of every patriot!

Prodigy books

Biographies

Abdul Kalam
Charles Darwin
Marie Curie
Visvesvaraya
Srinivasa Ramanujan
Newton
Einstein
James Watt
Jagdish Chandra Bose
Alexander Graham Bell
Gandhi
Jawaharlal Nehru
Mother Teresa
Ambedkar
Bhagat Sigh
Tipu Sultan
Rani of Jhansi
Akbar
Shivaji
Bharati
Martin Luther King
Alexander the Great
Napoleon
Adolf Hitler
Charlie Chaplin
Walt Disney
Bill Gates
Narayana Murthy

Classics Retold

Homer's Iliad
The Odyssey
The Tempest
Hamlet
The Merchant of Venice
Twelfth Night
Romeo and Juliet
Macbeth

Other Titles

The Universe
Hinduism
Global Warming
Abraham Lincoln
The New 7 wonders of the World
Life
Tsunami
Dinosaurs
Ganga
World War II
Madras - Chennai
Exam Tips
The Internet

www.ingramcontent.com/pod-product-compliance
Ingram Content Group UK Ltd.
Pitfield, Milton Keynes, MK11 3LW, UK
UKHW040003200726
13854UKWH00001B/19

9 788184 931921